A Girl's Guide to

MONEY

A Girl's Guide to
MONEY

Make the Rent, Control Your Credit Cards, Afford a Car, Pay Your Cell Bill, and Still Have Money for Shopping Sprees and Nights on the Town

Laura Brady

Ulysses Press

Published in the United States by
Ulysses Press
P.O. Box 3440
Berkeley, CA 94703
www.ulyssespress.com

10 9 8 7 6 5 4 3 2 1

Created and conceived by
Axis Publishing Ltd
8c Accommodation Road
London NW11 8ED
www.axispublishing.co.uk

Library of Congress Control Number
200411978

ISBN 1-56975-459-4

Creative Director: Siân Keogh
Art Director: Clare Reynolds
Editorial Director: Anne Yelland
Managing Editor: Conor Kilgallon
Illustrations: Marie Simpson
Production Controller: Jo Ryan

Printed in China

Distributed in the United States by
Publishers Group West

contents

introduction

*D*ealing with money is something that everyone *needs help with, but this guide has been written strictly with girls in mind.*

Although it's great to live in an age where females can be self-sufficient, this also means earning enough money to pay our own taxes, bills, and mortgages. Us girls also live independently which—single or not—means going out with our own friends. But of course this also means spending money in bars, restaurants, and movie theaters.

We are lucky to have the option of around-the-clock shopping, but this also means we are faced with more temptation than ever before to spend money.

Getting access to what you want is also easier than ever—you can wear today, pay tomorrow. But this shopping method means paying high interest rates and racking up big debts for the future.

In short, it can be a very expensive world. But the good news is that it is completely possible to live happily on your earnings without getting in debt and without forfeiting what you need. In fact, *A Girl's Guide to Money* and a little bit of determination are all you need.

bank on it!

1

Keeping money stashed under the mattress is, these days, a practice confined to the likes of criminals and people over 90. For the rest of us, the right checking account will represent the heartbeat of our finances...and that's something you can bank on.

time for
checking?

*I*f, to you, the term "personal finance" means an old bank book from the 1980s, it's time to get up to date with a checking account.

There are hundreds of these accounts to choose from so be sure to opt for one that is right for you.

the personal touch

If you value face-to-face contact, look at opening one of the checking accounts offered by a banking center situated close to your home or office.

phone or internet?

If you like to talk your finances through on the phone, there are several telephone banks to choose from. And if you are a time-poor Internet junkie, why not do everything online?

Take a look at the different kinds of checking accounts
before deciding which one is for you:

basic checking:

For those who use their checking account only for bill
paying and daily expenses, this pays little interest.

interest-bearing:

In return for higher interest payments, this account
requires a greater deposit to open. It may also charge
high monthly service fees.

express:

This type of checking is for those who are always
on the go, accessing their accounts via the ATM,
telephone, or Internet. Although no monthly fees will
be levied, it's likely you'll be charged for using an ATM.

lifeline:

With small or no monthly fees, these accounts only
offer restricted check writing since they are aimed
at the low-income customer.

money market:

This account—for high earners—combines checking
with savings and/or investments.

age-old issues

*B*ank accounts are for everybody. The one you qualify for, though, will depend first on your age, then on your status and income.

under 18?

If you are under 18 and want an ATM card, the account will usually need to be linked to that of your parents. But if the chance of this lies anywhere between unlikely and impossible, you'll have to stick to your savings account until you actually reach your 18th birthday.

18 and over

This is when you qualify for a fully fledged checking account. It will offer a checkbook and a check card that you can use at the ATM or over the counter, but—in similarly adult style—will charge a small monthly maintenance fee for the privilege. This is waived if you manage to keep a certain amount in credit—usually around a healthy $750. You can also apply for a line of credit on your checking account, which—at a cost—will cover any overdrawn transactions by no more than you have agreed.

TOP TIP!

If you are in college there is a range of more sympathetic student checking accounts designed to reduce the pain of temporary poverty while you study. With one of these you can benefit from loans with deferred interest as well as waived maintenance fees and minimum balance requirements.

opening your account

*O*nce you have found the checking account that's right for you and your circumstances, you've done the hard work.

The easy part is getting it opened, which you can do online or in a branch office. Here is a checklist of what you will need to open an account online:

CHECKLIST!

1   Your Social Security number. ☐

2   Your current address and any others you have lived at in the past two years. ☐

3   Your driver's license number. ☐

4   Your employer's details. ☐

5   Your email address. ☐

6   A minimum deposit—usually between $25 and $100. This will have to be paid online so you may have to use a friend's or parent's credit or debit card and then pay them back. ☐

But if you feel more comfortable going in to a branch, put the following in a large envelope under your arm:

1. Your Social Security number.

2. Two forms of identification. At least one should be a photo ID, for example your passport or driver's license.

3. A minimum deposit—usually between $25 and $100.

Once this is all in order and your card is activated, you are ready to go.

TOP TIP!

Take a deep breath and tell yourself you are on the starting blocks to life-long financial control. This is your chance to start as you want to go on.

the ins and outs of
checking

If you look past the design of your check card and checkbook, no two checking accounts in the world will look the same.

Different amounts go in and out on different days and at different frequencies. It can all be a bit of a balancing act so now is the time to organize your checking account to work around you.

FIRST, COME TO GRIPS WITH THE TERMS:

direct deposits:

Any money that is paid directly into your checking account is called a direct deposit. Unfortunately, most people only have one direct deposit hitting their account each month and that is wages for a grueling four weeks' work!

automatic bill payments:

More unfortunate still is the fact that for each direct deposit, there will be several more automatic bill payments, sometimes called direct debits. These are specific amounts of money that are set up to leave your account on the same day every month.

scheduled transfers:

These are also expenditures but used to pay more voluntary commitments—such as another personal account.

TOP TIP!

Remember your account is your own. As the account holder you are the only person that can set up, change, or cancel any of the above transactions.

first things
first

*T*o organize what will be the monthly core activity of your checking account, the first thing you will need to do is total up your fixed income and expenditures each month.

Your list might look something like this:

money in!

Take-home pay from work:	$2000
TOTAL INCOME:	$2000

money out!

Rent/mortgage:	$600
House insurance:	$60
Car insurance:	$100
Gym:	$40
Savings:	$200
Long-term budget:	$75
TOTAL EXPENDITURES:	$1075

Now it's time to schedule the dates of your expenditures around your direct deposit. Try to ensure all payments come out on the same day...and choose this day according to when you get paid.

the dating game

Although it's not good to be paid in Week One of the month and have your automatic bill payments in Week Three, you also don't want your account to be debited right on payday as you run a small risk of your wages not arriving in time. So, for example, if you get paid on Day One of the month, organize your bills to go out on Day Two. Then when you reach Day Three, you are safe in the knowledge that the rest of the money can be labeled "Me."

TOP TIP!

It is crucial that "savings" is classified as a fixed expenditure. Getting into the habit of saving, no matter how much, is almost more important than the amount you save.

it's money girl,
but not as we know it

If your finances were to stay constantly in the black (in other words, in credit), this book would be half the size and half as popular.

But let's face it—borrowing money these days is as tempting as it is easy. Before you make any decisions though, come to grips with your different credit options and remember they all have one thing in common—the money is not yours!

> **"It's not a straightforward case of 'credit is bad.' It is only mismanaging or relying on credit that becomes a problem."**

credit cards:

To be approved for a credit card—or any other form of credit—your credit rating, also known as a FICO score (see pp. 112–113), will be looked at first. If this is good, you'll be given a spending limit, which will be set according to your earnings.

beware!

Credit cards carry two main dangers. Interest rates can be very high and there is no set time frame over which to pay the balance back. So although you will have to repay at least the interest each month, you could still be maxed out on your limit 10 years from now. Look at credit cards that come with zero interest for a certain time. If you keep transferring your balance while closing the old account, you could escape ever paying a cent above the cost of your purchases.

store cards:

These work the same way as credit cards although you can only spend on them in one store—or sometimes a group of stores.

beware!

Sales clerks often introduce their cards to you with the question: "Would you like to save 10 percent on this item today?" Your answer should be "No." Their interest rates are phenomenal and any mention of a "saving" is misleading. What's more likely is you'll wind up paying for the item 10 times over.

TOP TIP!

The difference between the amount you borrow and the total amount you repay on a loan with interest can be huge. So do your math first—that credit might not look so appealing...

overdrafts:

This is the name for the line of credit available on your checking account. To use it means your checking balance will be less than zero.

beware!

With many checking accounts the bank will levy a charge if you go into the red. You may also have to pay interest on the debit balance.

personal loans:

This is a set amount of money that you apply to borrow from a bank or loan company. You agree to repay the loan over a certain time frame—say five years—at a given interest rate. The money is then deposited into your account.

beware!

If a loan is deemed "flexible," it means you are able to re-borrow back to your limit at any time, leaving you going around in circles. Hefty charges can also be levied for paying the loan off in full.

you are **the boss**

It's up to you to control your finances, and this relies on regular monitoring.

Traditionally, checking accounts as well as credit cards come with a monthly statement that is sent to you in the mail. But this can often feel like reading yesterday's newspaper.

how often?

A good rule of thumb is to check your accounts with the same frequency with which you use them.

If this is daily, why not monitor your credit cards and checking account online? This method will be the most up-to-date so you'll be aware of the exact state of your finances before your trip to the mall!

If you are not online, there is always the phone. Bank and credit card call centers are often open 24/7 so you can call any time for an update. Telephone banking allows you to access all the information on your account that you can online. The only down side to these options to keep on top of your finances is that there are no excuses for not doing it!

keeping statements

Just because you have chosen to bank online, it doesn't mean you can't print off your statements like a regular account and organize them in a file. Having paper copies of your statements from the last, say, six months can give you peace of mind as well as providing proof of identity should you need it for a passport or mortgage.

TOP TIP!

It is worth thinking of your different pots of finance as a practice for having kids...they all need attention, a bit of discipline, and to cooperate with each other!

watch out!

A healthy checking account provides the basis for successful juggling of all of your finances. But in case you feel you might drop a ball, look out for the following potential pitfalls.

overlooking clearance times

Not all money going into your account will be available for you to use immediately. For example, if a rich aunt sends you a check for $400 and you deposit it that day, usually the first $100 can be withdrawn immediately. You will have to wait until the next day to access the rest. If it's a real fortune you are depositing, the check may be held until the bank verifies it is really intended for you.

Similarly, if a friend owes you money and transfers it into your account online, leave up to two days for it to become available.

not having enough funds...

...to meet your set monthly payments: This means you'll rub two parties the wrong way—the bank and the company you should have paid. You'll probably get charged at both ends as well as risk damage to your credit rating (see pp. 112–113). This is why you should be sure your expenditures leave your account right after you are paid and all on the same day, rather than spreading them across the month (see pp. 18–19).

sweeping it under the carpet

If it's been a while since you looked at your balance, the thought of it might literally make you ill. But bite the bullet and go ahead. After all, you can't improve a situation if you don't know what it is.

damn it, i've been
charged!

You've tried your best but you've incurred a bank charge. This will be debited directly from your checking account; the bank will inform you of this.

But don't let this be the end of the story. You can bet your bottom dollar that the staff at the bank haven't sat around a table and discussed your bank charge and why they should levy it. Everything is computerized and automatic so the only

person who will actually be aware of your
particular charge is you. Don't be afraid to call
the bank and ask about the charge—what
have you got to lose by trying?

hey! I didn't spend that!

If you are unlucky, you may see a transaction
on your account you know you didn't make—
someone may be fraudulently using your
account. Don't panic! Inform the bank
immediately and it will refund your money
(providing you are using your account correctly)
and will issue you with a new card.

why might I be charged?

- If you have spent funds in your account that
  have not yet cleared.
- If you have exceeded your overdraft limit.
- If you have written a check or paid a bill online
  and do not have the funds to cover it.

control 2 yourself

You can keep the sugar and spice, but "everything nice" is hard for a girl to turn down. In the real world though, nice things cost money and the only person footing the bill is YOU. So control what you spend now and save yourself a lifetime of playing catch-up...

adding up
the costs...

Here's a question for you—how much does a carton of eggs cost? What about a tank of gas? Or a can of soda?

Although it seems absurd, we have all bought standard items like these time and time again without being aware of their price tags. This is partly because, since the dawn of check and credit cards, we no longer have to count out money to pay. We just hand over a piece of plastic and sign whatever comes back to us.

This approach to spending has to go out the window if you want to be the boss of your money. So why not take a trip down to your local grocery store and really look at the cost of basic items? Write them down if you feel inclined. You will see that in fact, the same things can differ immensely in price. So by swapping the organic fruit for

TOP TIP!

Get back to basics and start using cash. If you use your check card the transaction will go through automatically, but if you only have $80 in cash for your groceries, you might have to put a few things back.

regular fruit or compromising on the "gourmet" yogurt, you could go home with many of the same items, having shaved dollars off the price.

comparison list

item	replacement	saving
	total saving	

unexpected
booby traps

We all have to grow up eventually. And when you get there you realize it's not the picnic you thought it was going to be. In childhood, you were supplied with everything you needed from vests to vegetables. But not anymore!

Remember when the most worrying thing about your own budget was that you had to wait a week until your next candy fix? And when debt was something complicated and boring that grown-ups talked about? It's only when you become fully independent that you start to marvel at how your parents managed with the money they had.

Here are the top 10 boring costs that, as an adult, you are now wholly responsible for:

1   A "sensible" winter coat

2   Taxes, of any description

3   Medical insurance and dentist bills

4   Necessary haircuts

5   Maintenance for the car

6   Veterinarian's bills

7   Any tuition fees

8   Glasses or contact lenses

9   Entrance fees—anything from the zoo to the movies

10 Work clothes

As a result of these expenses, the balance on your account can still look unhealthy even when you haven't got a closet full of new clothes to show for it. Hard to swallow, yes, but learning how to exercise your own financial control is paramount.

the benefits of a
budget

According to the dictionary, the word budget is defined as follows: "Financial plan for a period of time; money allocated for a specific purpose."

TOP TIP!

Manipulating the figures of your budget plan to make more pleasurable reading is like stealing money from your own purse.

To take a literal reading of this definition, the only situation in which you would not need to budget would be if you were a billionaire and had an endless supply of cash. Presumably, since you are reading this guide, this is a situation that does not apply so you will need to draw up a budget plan, which will be set according to your income and your expenditures.

Drawing up a budget on paper is as easy as planning a vigorous workout five times a week. But obviously in both cases it's the sticking to it that counts. That's why, before you draw up your budget, it is crucial to be honest with yourself. If, for example, your cell phone bill is between $70 and $90 a month, budget for $90. Just like going to the gym, if you don't set achievable goals, it's likely that you'll give up on the whole thing. When drawing up your budget plan, you might want to start by allotting a rough percentage of your take-home pay to different areas of your life. For example:

sample budget

Item	%
Home (mortgage or rent, bills, groceries, decorating, furniture, insurance...)	40 percent
Socializing (birthdays, dinners, parties, movies, etc...)	10 percent
Closet (shoes, clothes, accessories, coats, etc...)	10 percent
Debts (credit cards, loans, etc...)	10 percent
Savings (for everything from vacations to emergencies)	20 percent
Money for my purse (for everyday costs from a coffee to a tank of gas)	10 percent

budget
timeline

*B*udgeting is all very well but your expenditures are not set in stone. Many will be daily, some weekly, most monthly, and others yearly.

While there is no point trying to predict what you are going to spend to the cent in six months time, it is certainly worth keeping the different timelines in mind.

daily expenses:

Sometimes it seems all you have to do to spend money is get up in the morning. So on a micro scale, consider these day-to-day expenses in your budget:

Lunch	1	
Newspaper	2	
Coffee	3	
Travel fares/parking lot charge	4	
Possible drink after work	5	
Daily total		

weekly expenses:

These can really surprise you since they are overlooked both on a daily and a monthly basis. Weekly expenses, however, play as much a part in your budget as any other type of cost. Consider the following examples when you are drawing up your brutally honest budget plan:

Take out	1	
Cleaner	2	
Grocery shopping	3	
Exercise class	4	
Big weekend night out	5	
Gas	6	
Weekly total		

don't forget:

Your daily and weekly budgets in some ways are easier to monitor because you are more likely to be using cash for these items; and, at some point during the week, you will find your wallet is empty. If that happens earlier and earlier in the week, you are not counting all your expenses accurately and will need to revisit your budget.

monthly expenses:

This will become the most worn part of your budget since many costs are built around salaries—which are typically paid on a monthly basis. For this reason take what you can from your monthly income and put it aside for your long-term budget. Your monthly expenditure might therefore appear something like this:

Rent or mortgage	**1**	
Loan and credit card repayments	**2**	
Cell phone bill	**3**	
Gym membership	**4**	
Savings for long-term budget	**5**	
Other savings	**6**	
Monthly total		

don't forget:

Your monthly budget is likely to be the core activity of your checking account, so it's important to get it right. Schedule as much as you can on a monthly basis to streamline your account—and your life—but note the tip opposite.

annual expenses:

Although these expenses are the least frequent, they can also be the most painful. But if you have put enough aside from your monthly salary, you should be able to meet yearly costs such as the following:

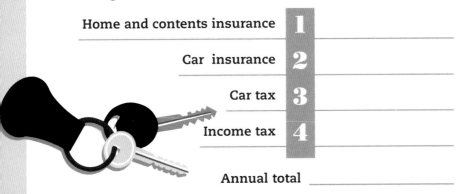

Home and contents insurance **1**	
Car insurance **2**	
Car tax **3**	
Income tax **4**	
Annual total	

don't forget:

Note on your annual budget the month that these bills are due, so that you can be sure funds are in your account to meet them. Car tax and insurance are likely to be due at the same time—the anniversary of buying the car—so that could prove an expensive month.

TOP TIP!

It works out cheaper to pay for things such as insurance upfront each year. Companies make money by charging interest if you choose to spread the premium over the year by paying on a monthly basis.

preparing for
occasions

One thing that is easy to overlook when drawing up your budget is special occasions, which— exciting as they are—can bulldoze all your good work. Plan ahead for the following:

birthdays

As well as presents, these often entail celebratory drinks and dinner. So be sensible. If you are spending a mint on a night out, go easy on the cost of the gift. Why not pitch in for something with friends? Far from being stingy, you are ensuring you'll have the money to attend the next birthday bash.

christmas

This is a pricey time of year for everyone. So before you race to the mall, credit card in tow, establish a maximum cost per gift with family and friends—$20 is ample. As well as returning with more imaginative Christmas presents, you can enjoy the festivities without worrying about how you're going to get through January.

weddings

Tears at weddings should be as much about cost as happiness! But you don't have to buy a brand new outfit every time. Designer dresses are best shared among friends. Let's face it—otherwise they are only worn once. Again, chip in with friends for a more thoughtful present and reduce the cost of hotels by sneaking a few pals in one room...

coping with
emergencies

*B*ut there are plenty of other events in life that you just can't plan for. These can be the ultimate stingers that really bring home the injustice of how much of your hard-earned cash has to go on things you resent.

Your car blows a tire, for example, or you get a speeding ticket. A window shatters, your vacuum cleaner dies, or you spill red wine down a friend's new white sofa. To deal with all these frustrating events, it will be up to you to find some money upfront. That's why it is crucial to have a cushion of cash to break your fall.

If you have stuck to your budget, you should have enough to cover

think ahead!

Emergencies are by definition unexpected, but there are things you can do to try to prevent them.

1	Check your car tires regularly—if you know they are worn you can plan to finance their replacement.
2	Look at warranty and insurance for expensive household items, such as washing machines and dryers. These could save you money in the long term.
3	Have expensive items of furniture protected against stains. It will cost extra upfront but will keep them looking good.
4	Read the instruction manuals for appliances to be sure you are using them correctly and following maintenance procedures.
5	Ask friends how long, in their experience, appliances last to give you an idea of when you might need to replace an item.
6	Schedule regular optician and dentist appointments; tiny problems fixed early will cost less than neglecting them.

unforeseen events such as these. It might be that your "Me" money amounts to nothing for the month or that you have to blow your long-term budget. But if the costs are spiraling out of control, it is better to dig into your savings—borrowing money is more expensive and should be a last resort.

TOP TIP!

Putting the cost of emergencies on credit increases their cost in the long run and ends up eating even further into your hard-earned salary.

come off it!
I just don't earn that much!

OK, so there are times when your budget will be a simple case of trying to fit a square peg into a round hole.

TAKE THE FOLLOWING SCENARIO:

It's Christmas and you land a speeding ticket on the way to the mall to do your wealth of shopping. You come home to find the washing machine has broken and realize that the cost of a new one is going to be very high. You are already over budget and have exhausted all avenues that will let you see Christmas through while remaining solvent. It's a situation that can get out of control, so short of conjuring money out of the air— **WHAT DO YOU DO?**

Although Shakespeare wrote in *Hamlet*, "Neither a borrower nor a lender be," he didn't have a washing machine. It's at times like this that you will have to bite the bullet and borrow. But if you have an option of borrowing at a zero interest rate—namely from The Bank of Mom and Dad—that's your first port of call. Don't be proud—everyone needs a little help from time to time. Just make sure you agree to a certain period over which you can pay the money back and buy them a bottle of wine to say thanks.

If you don't have this option, you'll have to pay by credit card or even take out a loan. But don't beat yourself up about this—all budgets must have a little flexibility and at least you won't have to worry about the washing machine for another 10 years.

TOP TIP!

Whether you use your credit card or get a loan depends on the size of the bill. If it's small enough to pay off quite fast—within six months, say—your credit card might be the best option, especially if you are still in a zero or low interest period.

payback time:

Draw up a repayment schedule with your parents—and stick to it. Just because it's Mom and Dad doesn't mean you should be casual about repayment. Although it hopefully won't be necessary, you might want to borrow from them in the future and they need to know you can make and honor a grown-up agreement.

budget
maintenance

*I*t might be the case that your budget is simply not working. You have tried to stick to it but are still putting things on your credit card or getting overdrawn at the end of each month.

It is crucial that at this point you do not admit defeat, claiming that: "I once tried a budget but it didn't work." Instead, look at exactly where things are coming unstuck by writing a list of everything you spend for a one-month period. If restaurants and bars appear often on your list, you might not like it, but there is your diagnosis.

If, however, you have not overspent on anything, look at how much you are putting away. It could be that, in your eagerness to remain solvent, you have forgotten that hard-earned money is to enjoy as well as to save for the future. So don't be too hard on yourself—a healthy balance to your budget means there is less chance of giving up on it.

...but so do costs

Also remember that salary and expenses tend to end up relative to one another. As well as paying more in taxes when you get a pay raise, you might decide you can now afford a bigger apartment or a new car. So before your extra cash evaporates into thin air, make a pact with yourself that with each pay raise you make at least one improvement to your financial situation. Increase the amount you save each month, or up the monthly payments on any outstanding loans or credit cards.

TOP TIP!

The more money you have, the more you can spend paying down a loan. This will not only shorten the term of the loan, but will reduce interest payments.

example:

Your revamped monthly budget following a pay raise might include the following headings:

Increase in monthly salary **1**	
Extra to savings **2**	
Extra to credit cards **3**	
New "Me" total	

"I said NO!"

Whatever your budget looks like, it will involve the word "No"—and this is often the biggest hurdle to get over. But to remain the boss of your finances, you must remain the boss of your life. Here are a few classic examples of when you should say "No"—and how:

1

when?

A friend is pleading with you to join her on a night out but your budget that week is already accounted for.

how?

Simply tell your friend that not only can you not afford it, you had planned a night in. Invite her over but do not be moved. If she can't respect your decision, why are you friends anyway?

when?

A work colleague has asked to borrow more money when they still haven't repaid you from the last time.

how?

Use this as an opportunity for a "joke." Try saying: "Sure! Give me back the $20 you owe me and you can re-borrow that!" Remember it is they—not you—who should feel embarrassed.

when?

You are cornered on the street by a charity worker, asking you to donate a certain amount of money each month from your checking account.

how?

Simply say you admire what they are doing but personally cannot afford to help regardless of the amount. Repeat it 10 times if you have to. Also keep in mind it is their job to pressure people. Plus that they won't remember you because over 90 percent of the people they stop also say "No."

danger
zones

*T*here are times, however, that—although you know you should say no and protect your budget—you go ahead regardless.

This is where you can watch all the hard work that you have put in over the months come undone over the course of a weekend. Watch out for the following scenarios:

you are with someone...

...who is careful with their own money. With certain people you seem to spend a fortune. Be prepared for this in advance— don't be embarrassed to say if it is not your turn or to ask for half of the cab fare. If you go out with that "set amount," you can also say that you have run out of money.

you are miserable

Just like having that extra slice of chocolate cake, buying those shoes if you can't afford to will only make you feel more down. See the cloud coming and be prepared to fight the urge.

you are already overdrawn

Somehow, money in your pocket seems worth more than the money available on credit. In fact, it is worth just the same. Keep away from the "drop in the ocean" attitude that occurs when the less money you have, the more inclined you are to spend.

you are trying to make friends

When you first go to college or start a new job, it's tempting to spend more on nights out in an attempt to be liked. But there is no such thing as a "quick fix" friend, even if you are at the bar all night buying the drinks. So don't bother—it's a waste of time and money.

you are drunk!

After a few white wines, it's easy to pull bills out of your purse like they are nothing but paper. Go out with a set amount and go home when it is gone.

on top of it all

Although budgeting seems like a lot of hard work, the rewards you will reap are priceless. When you feel in control of your finances, you'll also feel on top of other areas of your life, including your work and relationships. Being solvent and having some money to fall back on is also empowering. It means you are 100 percent independent and a girl who can afford to make her own decisions...because owing no one means answering to no one.

shop
until you stop

3

Store windows seem to emit a magnetic draw to us girls. To walk past without stopping—and then to resist the urge to venture inside—takes a huge amount of pull in the opposite direction. But the good news is you can cure this addiction in a few easy stages...and still be happy at the end of the day.

STAGE ONE:
don't believe
the hype

M ost young women care a great deal about their appearance—to the absolute delight of fat-cat advertising executives across the world.

After all, it means that any product from cellulite remover to anti-wrinkle cream to diet books to stay-on-all-night lipsticks are pretty easy to sell. Simply give the item a trendy image, show a beautiful model using it on television, and then tell lots of impressionable young women that they also need this product to look good. The first stage of coming to grips with your shopping addiction it to realize that this is absolute nonsense!

TOP TIP!

If you ever get fed up with questioning yourself each time you want to splurge on a gimmicky beauty product, smile and remind yourself it's "because you're worth it!"

cost-per-wear examples

1
One pair of classic designer jeans = $150
Wear them four times a week for two years = 416 wears
Cost per wear = 36 cents
Value = 10/10

2
One pair of bright yellow stilettos = $45
Wear them three times before injuring ankle = 3 wears
Cost per wear = $15
Value = 2/10

3
One fashionable winter coat = $175
Wear frequently over one winter = 122 wears
Cost per wear = $1.43
Value = 7/10

4
One designer purse = $150
Use every day for one year = 365 uses
Cost per use = 41 cents
Value = 10/10

STAGE THREE:
making the most of
what you have

Applying this rule of life to your closet can save you a fortune. So before you take off for the mall take a look at what you already have.

Remember, clothes can often spend a long time in the laundry or on the ironing pile. There might also be several garments in a heap at the bottom of your closet waiting to be dry-cleaned or some shoes you have written off just because the heels have worn down. So wash, iron, dry-clean, repair, and re-heel. Then hang everything back in your closet in a different order. Try organizing things by color, season, or into categories of skirts, pants, tops, and so on. Then look again at your closet in its entirety and you might be pleasantly surprised that you've got more than you thought.

accessorize

Remember that a new look does not necessarily mean that you have to head out to the mall to buy new clothes. Cheap accessories such as earrings, belts, scarves, and bangles can transform an old outfit. Even a new nail polish or lip gloss can provide a sufficient "fashion fix" for the month. So while assessing your existing closet, consider how a few well-chosen accessories could give it the renewed life it's screaming out for. You could get your shopping bill down to a fraction of the price.

TOP TIP!

Accessories are cheap only if you don't go overboard. Go out with a set amount and don't exceed it. If you have any money left over, add it to next month's "fashion fix." You may be pleasantly surprised at how little you can spend.

i really need...

You can ensure you buy the right things by filtering down what you want to what you really need. For example:

I want	a pair of red high-heeled boots
I need	a pair of high-heeled boots
I really need	a pair of boots I can walk in and wear through winter

STAGE FOUR:
making the most of what
your friends have

O K, so it's not one of Aesop's Fables but in these times of great expense using what your friends have—and returning the favor—can benefit everyone.

As long as all your girlfriends are willing, having a back-stage pass to each other's closets can multiply your selection of clothes by five or six.

Although you and your girlfriends will be different shapes and sizes, things like wraps, jackets, bags, and jewelry often transcend these differences. And borrowing rather than buying can save you all a fortune.

TOP TIP!

As soon as your back-stage pass is abused, the arrangement will fall apart. So make it a rule that all items are returned promptly—washed and ironed or even dry-cleaned.

the right occasions

Obviously this doesn't mean showing up at your buddy's house before work one day because you feel like wearing a different outfit. But there will be occasions where borrowing is the only way forward.

take the following:

weddings

Formal wear is often required here. It is usually expensive and worn just once so find out who has something you can borrow.

vacations

It's unlikely you'll all be going at the same time so make use of each other's sarongs, flip-flops, and even bags.

dates

When you are looking for that all-important knock-him-dead number a friend may have the very dress hanging in her closet just waiting to be put to good use.

clothes-swap parties

Let's face it, around 40 percent of the contents of every girl's closet is more or less unused. Perhaps you had been optimistic with the size of some pants you bought and find wearing them uncomfortable. And because they don't fit, they don't make you feel great. Or maybe that headscarf seemed like a good idea at the time but now it seems like a different head that chose it.

Alternatively, you might just be plain bored with the sight of everything you can see in your closet. That's why, although the idea of a clothes-swap party might seem a little childish, as long as you are on a budget its benefits are timeless. After all, new eyes on old clothes can give them a far greater life span. And you get to enjoy the bonus of a cheap night in with the girls, too. So invite as many girlfriends as you can muster together in the comfort of your own home, and get going.

TOP TIP!

Don't risk a friendship over an old shirt—in other words, only invite friends you know are going to play fair in terms of swapping clothes of equal value. If you feel you're being offered an unfair trade, you can always say no.

checklist...

What you will need for your clothes-swap party:

1 A minimum of four people is best, and if you are different sizes, remember it is not just clothes that cost money—bring along your accessories too.

2 Drinks. A fundamental requirement of any good party.

3 An empty house—a clothes-swap party is no place for boyfriends, husbands, or parents. All in attendance must have the same interests at heart.

4 Clothes. Try to all bring a reasonable amount—say one bagful each. Remember if you don't see anything you like you don't have to swap.

STAGE FIVE:
overcoming
sale seduction

*S*tores would have us believe that the idea of a sale is to save customers' money. Actually, the real purpose of a sale is to make the store more money.

Going shopping without a plan when the sales are on is asking for trouble. The more you drift around the stores, the more likely you are to impulse buy and blow your budget. Buying one item you really need full price may cost less than buying two or three "bargains" you are never going to wear.

Not only do stores still net way above what they actually pay for the garments from the manufacturers—even when sold at a reduced price—but sales are often used to sell off last season's merchandise, which would have to be disposed of anyway.

In addition, stores actually take advantage of their sales by bringing in cheap odds and ends that they would not normally stock, tagging them with a "mark down" price and selling them along with all the other remains. So just because you see something with a red "reduced" label on it, don't be fooled into thinking you must have a bargain—in many cases, you may not. Instead, revert to the checklist on pp. 60–61 to decide if you really need it.

the classic sale trap!

All too often, the clothes that you might be looking to replace at your clothes-swap party are the products of a sale—and this is no coincidence. Not only are sale goods usually second-rate, it is often unlikely you would have bought them at all had they not been so cheap. But such is the effect of a sale that even the most prudent shoppers can go astray. So remember, if you leave the store with a bagful of "bargains" you'll never wear, it's only the store owner that's happy.

successful sale-ing!

The best way to get real bargains in the sales is to know to the nearest cent what the item costs full-price and aim for at least a 50 percent discount. Get to the store on the first day, buy it, and leave.

STAGE SIX:
controlling
your flicking and clicking

*I*ronically, shopping these days doesn't necessarily mean going to the mall. You can just as easily mail order or buy online. But this method comes with its own set of dangers.

Firstly, there's the sheer ease of it. Flicking through the pages of a catalog is quite therapeutic. And if you are bored stiff at work, checking out the latest fashion collections online can seem fascinating. Then there is the absence of any physical cash from the transaction. This can create the feeling that you are not really spending money—or at best that you'll figure it out later.

it will catch up with you!

And with some mail-order products you can indeed deal with the payment later. However, this means a hefty interest rate and if you miss or are late with even one payment, it's a fast way to damage your FICO score.

Although a shopping website often requires your card details so it can debit your account immediately, it can also provide the option of charging the items to your store card. This is the biggest no-no of all, as the money you are then spending does not even belong to you! So opt for the bigger buzz that on-foot shopping offers and shun the complexities of mail order and online shopping altogether.

BEWARE!

While shopping online at work you are usually spending more than you are being paid to be there.

when to shop online

Shop online for items like discounted books and DVDs where you can see the reduction—and shipping is free.

when not to shop online

Avoid online shopping from companies that do not have a national reputation, that don't take returns, and that don't allow you to change your mind.

ordering from abroad

The comfort and ease of online shopping can also conceal some traps if you don't quite know what you're doing. Often, when buying goods from a different country, the price you see may not include import duty or local taxes. These are costs you may be liable to pay when goods cross an international or state border. Unfortunately, since you are buying online you do not benefit from the personal allowance that

hidden extras

1 Sales tax that you pay on everything, but which may not feature in the price.

2 Import duty is the tax that you are charged for bringing goods across an international border.

3 Other taxes, such as state tax, if you are buying from a different state.

4 Handling fees, which the retailer might charge you for dealing with your "difficult" order.

5 Shipping costs are the cost of physically getting the package to your home.

you would if you carried them personally. In short, this means you could end up paying tax on something as small as a new bikini.

getting it there

Don't forget that your online purchase will have to be sent to you, which often means paying shipping costs as well, so that bikini could end up costing a small fortune. Although you'll not escape duty as it is calculated on the total value of goods, why not save on shipping costs by teaming up with friends and placing one mass order? Alternatively, avoiding shopping sites altogether is even cheaper.

returns

It is also worth remembering that if you change your mind, most companies will expect you to pay to send the item back and it is in your best interest to send it guaranteed delivery— more expense for you.

TOP TIP!

Be careful if using public computers to pay for goods online. Always ensure you log off and be discreet when entering your details. Also remember to stick to well-established websites for Internet purchases.

STAGE SEVEN:
signing
savvy

These days it is easy to "have now and pay later." You can sport a brand new outfit today while yesterday's bill still sits on a store card or credit card, accumulating interest.

However, according to some stores—often those that sell homeware or expensive electrical goods—you can put your bill on credit and pay "nothing in interest for the next six months." Sure, you'll need to qualify for a line of credit, but then it's easy, right?

Wrong! Until you pay off the balance (which you can do at any time over the interest-free period), you will have to make six monthly payments which usually still incorporate interest. The total interest paid will then be refunded to you only if you pay the total balance back within the six months agreed. But if, as the store is hoping, you fail to pay up in time, you will be whacked

now voyager

4

It's good for a girl to experience as much of the big, bad world as she can. So any money spent on it is likely to be worth every cent. But coming to grips with some finance-savvy travel facts before the plane's wheels leave the runway can make your journey both cheaper and safer.

the shrinking
world...

W hen our grandparents were our age, to travel abroad meant they were either very wealthy or extremely lucky. It took years of saving and planning and they even had to turn up wearing their best gear for the journey.

But today, the world is at our fingertips. As we arrive in our droves at airports wearing comfortable tracksuits, we take it for granted that we can take off almost anywhere—at prices that are within the realms of extreme affordability, if you do your homework on fares and are prepared to accept some unsociable traveling schedules.

So whether you want a 10-day girly vacation, a romantic break with your partner, or a year's round-the-globe trip to search your soul, the good news is that there are ways of doing it without putting too big a dent in your checking account.

...and the shrinking cost of seeing it

The travel industry has become so huge that competition is driving prices way down. As well as lots of "working abroad" schemes—which mean you could support yourself when you get there if you want to—there are also companies that offer heavily discounted travel for students or for those under a certain age.

airline online

And there are extraordinarily cheap flights and deals to be found on the Internet. Online companies can often deliver better value to customers since they have fewer overheads—such as office space—to pay for. Always search around to find the best possible offer. The first thing you find is seldom the best.

the right
timing?

Unfortunately, the issue of timing when traveling goes beyond simply adjusting your watch as you come in to land.

When planning a vacation, think carefully about when it is going to fit best into your life. Try to organize any short breaks—whether a weekend skiing or two weeks in the sun—so you have to take the least possible days off work. This is especially important if you are your own boss since time off equals lost revenue. And if you're looking for something longer term, like a year's globetrotting, bear in mind that although a year away probably won't make any difference to your long-term career progress, taking it at the wrong time might.

Whatever you decide, take your time and try to consider all factors, including the financial consequences on your return from your time away, as well as the financial requirements of getting there and staying there in the first place!

it's now or never

Ironically, it's often when you have the least money that your opportunity to travel is at its peak—before mortgages and kids start to take their toll. So sometimes it's best just to go for it, perhaps before you even start on the career ladder. Once you have your travel costs covered you don't need a fortune because the trip could be budget all the way. The real purpose of going is to learn about the world, other people, and—of course— yourself...all of which costs next to nothing. Of course, it's never too late to travel, whatever your life situation, and the same cost-cutting tips always apply, no matter what your plans (see pp. 88–89).

TOP TIP!

Settling into a career, getting a mortgage, and falling in love are the three life situations least conducive with traveling the world. So why not pack up and go before they happen or before you get in any deeper than you already are?

making the journey and
cutting the costs

O nce you have decided that you are going to get away for a while, you'll need to be sensible and plan how to do it within your budget, however extensive—or not—that may actually be.

booking the flights

Make sure you add tax onto the price of any flights you find (as well as possible administration fees) to get a true total cost. You can often get the best offers if you take a last-minute deal or if you can be flexible about exactly what day and at what time you travel, and even which airport you depart from. And again, be sure to shop around for the best deal.

allocation on arrival

If you are going for a short-term visit, you can save money by securing your accommodation when you get there. Obviously this is a gamble but it's one you might get lucky on.

travel to the airport

Leaving your car at an airport parking lot can sometimes cost nearly as much as the vacation itself, so compare prices of public transport and cabs or, better still, see if you can get a friend or parent to take you.

don't go crazy on duty-free

Just because it's cheap, is it really the right time to buy a new perfume? Wouldn't you be better off saving your money for more fun at your destination?

phone cards

Cell phones are handy as lifelines but using them from abroad will cost a fortune. If you want to call home, buy an international phone card. Not only will the calls be cheaper, but the cost is dealt with upfront.

money matters
abroad

Cutting any travel off short because of money issues would be infuriating. So it's worth making a thorough attempt at getting all your finances straight before you leave for pastures new.

currency exchange

TOP TIP!

Pick up a currency converter from your local travel agent. It makes more sense when you can see what you are spending in dollars—and it might make you think twice before you spend it!

You will need to switch some dollars for the currency of the country you are visiting. It's best to check the exchange rates regularly when you want to change your money since you will get more for your dollar one day than you will on another. Also, look for places that do not charge commission on your currency exchange and leave enough time for them to order the currency you require if necessary.

U.S. dollars

Bear in mind that some countries will be as happy to accept U.S. dollars as their own currency. Find out if this is the case where you're headed—you will save money by not paying commission on the currency exchange.

traveler's checks

When going on vacation, it is sensible to take about two thirds of your total spending money in traveler's checks. Unlike cash, if they are lost or stolen they can be easily canceled. Make sure, however, that you sign them—once only—as soon as you receive them. Otherwise, they could be used by anyone!

withdrawing money

You can withdraw cash from an ATM machine anywhere in the world with most check cards. Although this will involve a charge per withdrawal, at least your money is being kept safely in the bank (away from any potential pickpockets)—and it arrives in the local currency.

using credit cards abroad

Most places around the world will accept a variety of credit cards, so these are invaluable tools. However, pay off as much outstanding debt on your cards as possible before you leave, so plenty of credit is available. This means you can also avoid using your credit card to withdraw cash at an ATM, where a high fee is charged for each withdrawal.

the value of cash

Don't always rely on your plastic. You might find that your Visa is useless (as well as embarrassing) when trying to make a donation to a Mongolian monastery, for example. Always have some cash in the local currency.

dealing with your home affairs

If you have existing debt at home that is paid by a monthly deduction from your checking account, ensure there are enough funds in your account to cover your repayments for the time you are away. Consider opening a separate "travel account" so you know where you stand each step of the way. This means no nasty dents in your travel money if a bill that slipped your mind suddenly gets debited from your checking account.

using the web

Make use of Internet banking from wherever you are in the world—you should be able to find an Internet café in most cities, so do this before you head off into the wilds. This will help you to be sure your home account is well-oiled and operating properly.

safety first

Tourists carrying valuables, such as cash, phones, and passports are usually unfamiliar with their surroundings and off their guard—a great combination for thieves and muggers!

To really relax on your trip, take a few safety precautions to ensure you are not just another police statistic.

1

Don't carry too much in cash: Enough to cover things like drinks, snacks, and entrance fees is plenty.

2

Use a sensible bag: It might not be the coolest of accessories but put your spending money in something that straps round your waist. You can often buy ones to wear under your clothing to store valuable documents, like your passport and traveler's checks.

3

Pay by credit card when you can: These (unlike cash) can be cancelled if stolen, and if someone is using your card, your loss will be refunded.

4

Learn the value of the currency: Holding your hand out to a street vendor waiting for them to take what they are owed from a fistful of notes is asking for trouble.

5

Look confident: Unfolding a map the size of a sheet with a worried look on your face is going to make you a prime target for mugging. Buy a handy size guide, sit down for a coffee, and plan your route more subtly.

6

Use a safe: Most accommodation offers safes that you can rent. Lock up all valuables here, especially your passport and some traveler's checks.

covering yourself...

You never know what lies ahead when you are at home, never mind when you're roaming an unfamiliar continent. That's why taking travel insurance before you depart is absolutely crucial. The right insurance will cover everything from lost baggage to medical bills to flight delays. Some credit card companies include travel

what you can insure against

These are the minimum basics which must be covered by any policy you choose:

1 Medical insurance for any doctor's bills, medicines, hospitalization, and air evacuation in an emergency.

2 Lost property, including lost or late-arriving baggage, and lost or stolen goods such as cameras, CD players, and bags.

3 Delays and cancellations, including the cost of alternative transport, missed connections, and overnight hotel stops.

4 Trip cancellation—if a family or domestic emergency means you can't catch your first flight after all.

5 A 14-day "cooling off" period if you've made the wrong decision—as long as you haven't traveled yet.

insurance as part of their package, so call yours to check if you are already covered—and exactly what for. Alternatively, there is a wide range of travel insurance products on the Internet at very competitive rates. Taking a policy from your local travel agent may seem simpler but you will be likely to pay a premium.

...and exposing nothing!

With insurance, just going for the cheapest option is not always the best idea. If you are traveling abroad and lose all your money, having a comprehensive policy is far more important. So you'll have to find out exactly what you are covered for and go through the small print very carefully. For example, some policies only cover delays from your "original departure point." This means that although you would be compensated for the delay of your first flight, it would then be up to you to cover the costs of missing any connecting flights and staying in a hotel. Don't wait until it is too late to find out about simple loopholes like this one.

TOP TIP!

Always look at how and when the insurance company will pay if you make a claim. It might be acceptable to claim for a delayed flight when you get home but if you get all your money stolen you need it in your account right away to continue your trip.

rescue remedy 5

People who say, "Money doesn't matter" probably don't need to worry too much about it. But when you lay awake at night worrying about mounting bills that you can't pay, money matters a lot. Most people with money problems seek too little help too late. The simple steps in this chapter will make sure you don't become one of them...

why things go
wrong

W ith all the good will and budgeting in the world, people still find themselves in some financial hot spots from time to time.

In a lot of cases things can start to go wrong as a result of unforeseen circumstances. This could mean anything from losing your job, to carrying out emergency home repairs, to getting a divorce, to losing a fortune in the stock market. These are all situations that can lead to excessive debt, which can mean late payments, which can lead to a damaged FICO score and beyond…

ostriches and sand

The other reason why things go wrong of course is that—being human—we sometimes spend beyond our means and fall into a state of financial complacency. Then, when you have gotten to the point where the sight of your finances makes you feel sick, a common but irrational cure is to go on spending and stick your head in the sand like an ostrich. This haven of delusion lasts for a while, but eventually—and inevitably—the guilt sets in, the credit runs out, and we suddenly find ourselves running our lives around the search for money.

losing your job

When you lose your job, the most important things you can do revolve around damage control:

1 Don't panic. Redo your resume, get online, buy relevant papers and journals, and get yourself right back in the job market.

2 Don't be proud. Now is the time to ask family and friends for financial help, if needed.

3 Ask credit card companies if you can pay interest-only for three months, while you get another job.

4 If paying bills is going to be difficult, consider a temporary job, but keep hours flexible so you can attend interviews.

5 Cut your "Me" money to zero until you get another job. Your social life can revolve around home for a while.

STEP ONE:
addressing
the problem

*S*tuck in a sticky web of money problems is not a nice place to be, so denying you are there at all can seem like a good idea.

But to even start back on the road toward financial health, you'll have to admit you have a problem in the first place—and that something needs to be done about it.

TOP TIP!

Don't approach your parents with the "I'm not a child" mindset. To your parents, you are a child—their child— and chances are they will be pleased you felt you could come to them— even if they can't help you financially.

swallowing your pride

Your good friends and family could well be the first people to call on for help. Lay out in front of them your complete unabridged financial situation and see if anyone can offer you a loan. But even if it's your own Mom who comes through, it is crucial to set down some terms and conditions about your repayments—because fighting over money is a million times worse than just having trouble with it.

getting things in perspective

Even if your friends and family are unable to provide financial aid, just being offered a shoulder to cry on and an ear to bend can remind you that, on the list of life's problems, money has to be pretty near the bottom. Having your life, health, and the support of your family and friends are the only things that really matter. You will probably always have food and shelter and the days when you would have been thrown in the nearest debtors' prison are long gone. So try not to panic—it will help you think more clearly.

get it down on paper?

This is the worst possible time for ignoring your debts and commitments, so write everything down logically.

1 List your fixed monthly expenditures, including loan repayments; separately list outstanding balances on credit cards.

2 Write down the balance of your checking account, the total of your savings, and any other funds you could draw upon.

TOP TIP!

The Internet is a good place to find a contact for a reputable debt helpline. But beware if there is any mention on the company's homepage of borrowing further money, since this is highly unlikely to be the sort of help you need.

somewhere to turn

If you feel that there is no one close you are willing or able to talk to, there is a wide range of debt counselors out there—many of whom can be reached on a toll-free phone number. Helplines like these are very busy these days, since the level of personal debt continues to increase year after year and the labor market fluctuates. The counselors will have heard it all 100 times before and at levels 100 times worse than your own, so it can sometimes be refreshing and constructive to seek the advice of this outside support.

drawing the line

These avenues of support, however, are completely different to debt consolidation companies. Steer well clear of any "support line" that is offering money as a solution to your debt problems. Firstly, it is unlikely to be a reputable company, which will mean you have no legal recourse should things go wrong. Secondly, the interest rates charged will be much higher than the regular bank rates since they prey on people's desperation to "get it fixed." And no money situation is too desperate to devise your own recovery plan, with the advice and support of a counselor, family, or friends.

people who can help

1	Your parents may be sympathetic even if they can't help.
2	"Rich" relatives may be able to help financially.
3	Former teachers may be able to offer advice.
4	The local library should have information and leaflets.
5	A bank manager will know the best ways to attack debt.
6	A financial advisor can help you see the bigger picture.
7	An accountant can help you draw up a full list of debts.
8	A debt counselor can be recommended by your bank.
9	A debt counseling helpline can provide someone to talk to.
10	Internet debt counselors may offer free advice.

STEP TWO:

drawing up a
recovery plan

Recovery plans involve being honest and getting practical. Try the following suggestions.

say "no" to yourself and others

Continuing to shop is not an option. If you can't trust yourself, simply don't let yourself go anywhere near a mall. Also, explain to friends that you are socially "on hold." Good friends will understand.

cut up the credit cards

It's time to drop the "I'll keep the credit card for emergencies," line. Your account is probably now at its limit anyway and further debt is not an option. So cut up all your cards—including store cards—into small pieces, and put them in the trash.

draw up a list of priorities

Otherwise known as "keeping the wolves from your door," prioritize who needs paying first. These people or organizations will probably be those to whom you owe most money (and who are charging the most interest), such as banks and credit card companies.

draw up an emergency budget

After meeting your priority debts, you won't be able to live off thin air. So draw up a revised budget to cover your other basic expenses. Rent or mortgage, bills, gas, and food should really be the only factors here.

STEP THREE:
taking action
sooner rather than later

*I*f worst comes to worst when drawing up your recovery plan, you might realize (with a wave of horror), that you do not have enough funds to pay the creditors you owe.

It is now more tempting than ever to stick your head back in the sand and wait for it all to disappear. But, at this point, there are two things you can be certain of:

1	**It won't just disappear.**
2	**Defaulting on credit commitments spells trouble.**

That's fine, but if you simply don't have the money, what do you do?

honesty is the best policy

Although companies that offer any form of credit appear to set their repayment schedules in stone, this is only to prevent borrowers from being relaxed about their commitments. By calling the creditor and explaining your situation, you are proving that you are not being relaxed about yours. Don't wait for the final notice before you do this though. The bottom line is that creditors want their money back and they would rather have it later than not at all. You just have to convince them that they will get it and agree to a workable repayment schedule.

TOP TIP!

There is no point giving creditors half the story— remember they have always heard a situation 100 times worse than your own.

"Presenting yourself as a responsible borrower who wants to meet their commitments will get you looked at far more favorably."

what next with creditors?

Creditors will help you, but not from the kindness of their hearts. Their policy is that some of their money back is better than none, so here are a couple of solutions you might be offered:

solutions to consider

1	**Reducing your repayments for a certain time period.**
2	**Paying just the interest on the debt for a certain time period.**

This means that you will be up-to-date with the minimum you owe the creditor, although you will not be reducing your overall balance.

It is very important to bear in mind though, that when you are asked what you can afford to repay, be honest and realistic—however small the amount.

meeting your payments

Set up revised deductions for the new payments on dates that you know are "safe," that is, your salary has been paid and there will be funds available. Cut down on everything else you have to in order to avoid defaulting on a payment.

keep on top of it

Check your bank balance daily to be sure there are no nasty surprises. This is going to be a long haul, but keeping on top of it now is the only way to future stability. Tell yourself that it will get easier—because it will.

it's not that bad

It is imperative that you fulfill your commitments to your new revised payment plan—that's why ensuring it is realistic in the first place is also crucial. But once it's in place and you are paying your way, you can sleep easy again. Creditors will leave you alone if they are safe in the knowledge that you are paying whatever has been agreed to on schedule.

TOP TIP!

During your negotiations, ensure that when you are able to make repayments in full again, you do so immediately. Being restricted to any reduced payment plan when you can afford more means paying over-the-top in interest.

STEP FOUR:
understanding your
FICO score

*F*ICO stands for Fair Isaac Company, which is the company that first developed the idea of using a credit score to determine the likelihood of credit users paying their bills.

You actually have three FICO scores, one from each of the credit bureaus, which are Equifax, Experian, and TransUnion. A potential creditor will look at any one of these (a mortgage company will usually look at all three) before it decides whether or not to lend to you.

TOP TIP!

However little money you have, defaults on your FICO score can and must be avoided.

what's included?

Your FICO score will list all credit opened in your name, your payment history of that credit, and your current payment status. The higher your score, the more chance you'll have of borrowing and the lower borrowing rates you'll be offered.

the importance of protecting your FICO score

Protecting your FICO score from the outset will make your life a whole lot easier. What you don't want is for creditors to see a string of defaulted payments. This will show you to be an irresponsible borrower and cause any future creditors to either charge you a fortune in interest or refuse to give you credit at all. So it is crucial—even if you are on a revised payment plan—that you make sure all payments are met.

see what they see?

You can get an estimate of your FICO score on the Internet, by filling out a questionnaire. You can also purchase online reports from all three bureaus, either from the bureau itself or from independent companies such as *www.myfico.com*. Fees and packages vary, so choose the one that best meets your needs, but do get all three scores since the bureaus don't share information.

what will damage my FICO score?

It's not just failing to meet payments that will have a negative effect your FICO score. The following situations might also cause you problems:

1

If you have not been at your current address or at your place of employment for very long...
Staying put at one address gives creditors peace of mind that they'll know where to contact you should they need to. And stable employment means regular money, which—in turn—is likely to translate into reliable and prompt payment.

2

If you have been slow in meeting payments...
Paying at the last possible opportunity hardly presents you as a conscientious borrower.

3

If you have no credit history at all...
It might seem unfair but the only reliable proof for creditors that you will make your payments is seeing that you have done it before. If you haven't, it will go against you.

4

If you have too many outstanding balances...
Using credit is one thing but living off it is another. If the creditor sees you have borrowed to maximum capacity, it will be concerned about where you'll go from there.

5

If there have been too many credit companies searching your file...
If you are seen to be constantly in search of credit, it is unlikely you really have the cash to fund your existing commitments—never mind another one.

effects of a bad FICO score

Along with regular credit cards, personal loans, and lines of credit, remember the term "credit" applies to anything from a cell phone contract to a mortgage. So in some circumstances, to be refused credit on the basis of a low FICO score can actually have an effect on the way you live your life. For example, if your score is very bad and you are refused even a check card from the bank for that reason, life in the 21st century could become quite difficult.

TOP TIP!

It is worth checking your FICO score regularly at *www.myfico.com*, although, unfortunately, checking all three scores will cost about $40.

STEP FIVE:
realizing there are still
doors open

M ost people's credit problems are pretty minor—
perhaps they have overlooked a couple of credit
card payments or been overdrawn a few times.

For cases like these, there are still doors
leading to further credit that remain open.
In fact, the sale of loans, credit cards, and
even mortgages to the many people
suffering with mild credit problems is big
business, so there's little need to be
backward about coming forward.

"non-conforming" credit

Certain creditors will agree to lend to
higher-risk borrowers. However, remember
at all times that they do not do this because
they happen to be charitable. They are often
small companies that operate outside
mainstream boundaries and—quite legally—
make their money from charging high-risk

TOP TIP!

Do anything in your
power to avoid
taking any kind of
expensive, "non-
conforming" credit.

high-risk borrowing

There are several reasons why you might not qualify for regular credit, but these problems can be rectified:

1	Rebuild your FICO score. This is the single most important way to get regular credit.
2	Get an accountant to look at your income and expenditures and start to file audited accounts. This is if you fail to qualify because your income is difficult to verify.
3	Play the waiting game. The longer you can avoid non-conforming credit, the less chance there is you might need it.
4	Shop around. If non-conforming credit is your only option, remember rates and terms vary widely.

borrowers higher interest rates than borrowers with good FICO scores would pay. Other catches can include a limited choice of options—perhaps you want a mortgage with a fixed rate of interest but have to pay a variable rate, for example. Alternatively, it could be that there is a charge levied if you want to leave the mortgage within a certain time frame, or perhaps there will be hefty upfront fees to take it in the first place.

STEP SIX:
rebuilding
your FICO score

*T*he first thing to realize when attempting to repair your FICO score is that—just like trying to lose weight—there are no real shortcuts.

It's important therefore to realize that the following tips must be employed over a considerable period of time:

1 Continue to keep paying your financial commitments on time and in full
This is the all-time greatest FICO score healer.

2 Keep credit revolving
A rolling stone gathers no moss so don't keep high balances sitting on cards—pay your debt down so you're seen as trying to reduce the balances.

3 Apply for some credit
If you do not have a credit history, apply for a credit card and pay it off in full each month to prove you are a responsible borrower.

4 **Do your loan shopping within a focused time period**
FICO scores distinguish between a search for a single loan (such as a car loan or mortgage) and a search for many new credit lines, partly by the length of time over which inquiries occur. Too many inquiries may look questionable—as if you're a credit risk to lenders.

5 **Transfer balances**
Consolidating expensive debt and keeping your balances moving looks positive.

don't be fooled

The following are often misconstrued as being beneficial to your FICO score but they actually make little difference:

1. Having a credit card with no balance.

2. Paying off balances in full and closing accounts.

TOP TIP!

You can't please all of the people all of the time...different creditors will look for different things when assessing your FICO score, so don't be upset if one company says "Yes" and one says "No."

STEP SEVEN:
taking matters back into
your own hands

*D*uring the course of your recovery plan and credit repair stint, you might want to look at additional methods of getting yourself back on track.

Any extra strength you can muster up to pull yourself out of this financial rut will really speed up your recovery process. Try the following options:

set up a new saving plan

No, this is not a joke. Putting even just $5 in a savings account every month can provide a real mental boost.

give yourself a weekly review

Monitoring your recovery progress regularly will ensure you stay on track and allow you to feel pleased with yourself for doing so.

exercise

It won't help your bank balance, but exercising does wonders for the mind. When your workout is done, you will feel you can take on the world.

ask for a pay raise

In today's world of work, if you don't ask you don't get, so get your case together and go for it.

look for pleasure in things that are free!

It's only since the world has become commercial that we assume we must spend money to have fun. But walks in the country, reading, cooking, writing, or watching a movie at home are all great activities that cost next to nothing.

TOP TIP!

Remember that any work for which you receive payment must be declared on your tax form. Take this into your calculations when you are figuring out how fast you will get back on financial track.

raising money fast

Why not even try to raise extra money? If you cast your mind back to when you were a little girl, you might remember that, in fact, you regularly used to devise money-making schemes. Often they amounted to a bad job of washing the family car or trying to sell your old toys from a booth on the driveway. When the gritty reality of grown-up poverty kicks in, why not revisit that childhood innovation? If there is ever a time when you need an extra income it's now and you might just remember how good it feels to earn rather than to spend.

"Necessity is the mother of invention... think big and small, get your friends involved—they may have ideas that you haven't thought of."

money-making schemes?

Some of the following ideas might require the support of a friend to make them fun as well as fruitful...

1	Take an evening job in a local bar or restaurant.
2	Do some babysitting or dog walking.
3	Look for freelance opportunities in your chosen profession (but make sure this doesn't lose you your job!).
4	Do some straightforward decorating for a friend or offer to do gardening (if you know what you're doing).
5	Hook up with a pal and sell your unwanted junk at a garage sale.
6	Return any unworn clothes to the store they came from and ask for your money back.

back on track

It's difficult but do-able. Tell yourself that the rewards are worth it—you can face the future confident and stress-free.

chapter six

the future 6
starts now

The future is an exciting prospect when you are both young and female—you can do whatever you want to do and have plenty of time to do it in. But a 21st-century girl has to be financially independent. This chapter explores how to look after yourself and your money now and for the rest of your life...

evaluating
your goals

*T*he first thing to ask yourself is what your financial objectives are and when you want to achieve them. Start by categorizing your goals into short, medium, and long-term to get an overall picture. They might look something like the following:

short-term goals

1	To keep within my budget.
2	To increase monthly repayments on my loan and credit card by a small amount.
3	To cut down on unnecessary spending.
4	To stop borrowing from friends.
5	To get into the habit of using cash instead of cards.

medium-term goals

1 To continue saving.

2 To get a pay raise within the next six months.

3 To ensure that my credit cards and loans are paid off in the next year.

4 To tackle my shopping addiction head on.

5 To pay into a retirement account.

long-term goals

1 To own my own house or condo.

2 To pay off my car.

3 To have enough money to open bank accounts for my kids.

4 To be the company director.

5 To live my life financially solvent.

making your money
work for you

*I*t's widely accepted that you have to work for your money but why shouldn't your money also be working for you? These days, there are plenty of ways you can ensure that it does:

taking an interest

Although it might not feel like it now, interest won't always be something that costs you. As your debit balances are replaced with credit balances, you'll be looking for high rates of interest instead of low. Start by looking at what your checking account is paying. None will make you a fortune but you want to see your money at least working harder than it would be sitting under the mattress. Look also for high interest on your savings account (see pp. 132–133 for more information).

TOP TIP!

If you can ever trust yourself to do it, paying your bills online just before you get paid will provide the highest possible balance on your checking account at any one time—meaning you benefit from maximum interest.

making the most of technology

Online accounts not only offer better interest rates, but also make life a lot easier when you want to move your money around. This means your money is doing what you tell it when you tell it, which—as well as more potential interest—means fewer potential charges.

benefits of online banking

1	You have instant access to your balance in real time any time of the day or night.
2	Your account is updated faster—you can see an ATM withdrawal within an hour on your computer.
3	Rates and charges vary but generally interest rates are higher and charges lower than regular accounts.
4	If the bank offers a personal finance program for your computer, you are well on the way to filling your tax return, saving you time.
5	If you have lots of bills to pay, it saves the hassle of writing checks and remembering to mail them.

packaging your debt

When you take out a mortgage, you'll have to make a choice about what "package" you want it to come in. Your main decision will usually be whether you want to take it over 15 or 30 years and whether you want a fixed

different mortgage packages

1   Adjustable rate mortgage (ARM): The interest rate changes periodically, based on a pre-selected index.

2   3/1, 5/1, 7/1, and 10/1 ARMs are adjustable rate mortgages in which the rate is fixed for 3, 5, 7, or 10 years respectively, but will vary after that.

3   Fixed rate mortgage: The interest rate will remain the same for the length of the mortgage.

4   7/23 and 5/25 mortgages are fixed rate mortgages, with one change of rate, after 7 and 5 years respectively.

5   With a biweekly payment mortgage, you make your monthly payment in two halves, which over the years saves you money in interest charges.

6   A graduated payment mortgage (GPM) is a type of flexible mortgage in which the payments increase for a certain period of time, then level off.

or adjustable rate of interest. It is always
sensible to take the shortest term possible
as you will be saving money in interest. But
the repayments on this will be higher, so do
your math and see what you can afford.

Whether you save more in interest
repayments by taking a fixed or an
adjustable interest rate is a gamble, since
the Federal Reserve System (the Fed)—on
which your mortgage rate is based—
fluctuates. Bear in mind you will pay a slight
premium for any fixed rate in return for the
peace of mind it offers.

TOP TIP!

Choose your
mortgage wisely
by considering your
own financial
situation rather
than just trying to
"outwit" the Fed—
because even
economic experts
can't be sure what's
around the corner.

offshore accounts

Opening a savings account in a different
country can bring tax advantages as well as
complete anonymity and first-class service
to your financial affairs. These days you do
not have to be a member of the wealthy
elite to open an offshore account—you
can even do it online—but most people
interested in this form of banking tend
to have a strong grip on their finances
at home first.

choosing the right
savings account

A savings account is a must when preparing for your future. There is a wide range to choose from but it's not just about the best interest rate—it's about the best rate for the account that suits you. Look at the following scenarios:

"I want a good rate of interest...
...but still need to be able to dip in and out of my account."

Look online for a regular savings account that offers high interest while allowing you to make withdrawals at short notice without charging you a penalty.

TOP TIP!

Make use of the staff at your local bank branch who should be happy to talk you through the many different savings options available.

"I want to pay...

...a regular installment into my savings account."

Some savings accounts offer premium rates of interest on the condition that you pay in a certain amount each month. If you fail to do this, the interest rate will fall...which provides a great incentive to keep saving.

"I don't want to pay...

...tax on the interest I earn on my savings account."

Although it doesn't seem fair, even the interest you earn on your savings is taxed at the rate of your usual tax code. But there are some savings accounts that will pay interest tax-free. These will impose a limit on the amount you can put in each year and you may incur a penalty for withdrawing funds.

"I don't want...

...access to my savings."

If you can't trust yourself to leave your savings alone, why not take out some bonds? Bonds only mature after a given amount of time and pay good rates of interest up until that point.

investing
wisely

*F*inancial investments sound as though they only concern stockbrokers. But the definition of investment—"A thing worth buying because it may be profitable in the future"—applies to everyone.

For long-term investment options then, why not try some of the following? The sooner you start investing, the more money you could potentially accrue.

buy some shares

When dabbling in shares for the first time, it's good to take advice from someone in the know. This could be a financial advisor, but bear in mind that the cost of this could outweigh the return on your money. For most novices investing only small amounts, the help of a clever friend or the financial papers would be enough. The idea is that you buy shares in a company that you think is going to grow. As the company grows, its share price will rise. A decade ago, for example, investing in a cell-phone firm or an Internet company would have been a good bet. But beware—stock values can go down.

get a retirement account

You won't be youthful and resilient forever so what you earn now will need to pay for your old age. The earlier you start paying into a retirement account, the trendier your ballroom dancing shoes will be in later life (or the more adventurous your senior citizens' travels—whatever your taste is!) so ask your employer about their retirement plans.

keep and buy potentially valuable items

Twenty years ago, no one ever dreamed that *Star Wars* merchandise, for example, would be valuable. So, make an educated guess at what you own that could hold the same surprises in store, and keep it (and its box) somewhere safe.

TOP TIP!

An investment is never guaranteed to make money. For this reason a good rule of thumb is to only ever invest what you can afford to lose.

buying your
first home

Buying your first home is probably the biggest and most expensive investment of your entire life. That's why it feels as though there will never be a time when you can really afford to do it.

But rest assured that almost everyone who embarks on that treacherous journey to home ownership suffers financial drought along the way.

But if house prices have climbed way beyond the realms of affordability in the area you want to buy, why not pair up with a friend or sibling? This way (if house prices rise—and they eventually will, even if it takes time) you can get some equity (the difference between the mortgage debt and house value) under your belt, and then plan to branch out alone in a few years. But before you take the plunge, take in the following home truths:

home truths

1 You'll be able to borrow more if there are two of you.

2 The greater the deposit you can save, the smaller a mortgage you'll need and the better rate of interest you will get.

3 It's not just about mortgages. Property tax, legal fees, and removal costs should all appear in any "affordability assessment."

4 With a fixed rate mortgage you'll pay more in interest but will know exactly what's leaving your checking account each month; whereas with an adjustable rate mortgage, you're likely to pay less but the amount can change at any time.

5 Making home improvements to your property can increase its short-term value by more than the improvements will cost you to carry out.

6 In the very long term, it is almost certain that by the time your mortgage is paid off, your home will be worth a lot more than you bought it for.

covering
yourself

As soon as you buy a property, you will be opening up another can of expenses—the most unavoidable being the right insurance policies. As a homeowner, here's what coverage you might need and why:

homeowner's insurance

This will protect the structure of your property and its contents from unforeseen events such as fire, theft, or adverse weather conditions.

WHY DO I NEED IT? If tragedy strikes and you are without this insurance, you could still be liable for a debt on something that no longer even exists.

TOP TIP!

Failing to tell the truth on any insurance application in an attempt to reduce your premium is as useful as shooting yourself in the foot. On claiming, if the details of the application are found to be inaccurate, the policy becomes void and—in return for all those monthly premiums—you receive nothing.

health insurance

Rather depressingly, if you contract one of a list of diseases, this insurance will pay for all or part of your outstanding mortgage. It is usually available through your employer.

WHY DO I NEED IT? Quite simply, if you are very ill, you can no longer earn money to pay for your home.

life insurance

Even more depressing is this product, which will pay your beneficiary a lump sum of money if you die. If you smoke, you pose a greater risk and will pay a higher premium. So there's another reason to stop.

WHY DO I NEED IT? If you have dependents (in other words, kids), they can use the money to pay off the mortgage and other expenses when you're gone.

mortgage unemployment insurance

This will cover your monthly mortgage repayments for a given amount of time if you lose your job through no fault of your own.

WHY DO I NEED IT? If your monthly paycheck stops dead in its tracks and you have no savings, your mortgage repayments still need to be met.

realizing the importance of
financial control

Whether it is earned, spent, borrowed, lent, saved, wasted, craved, or despised, both the purpose and the importance of money is often widely misinterpreted.

Some people believe that money is the key to happiness, yet one look at the growing number of Lottery winners who end up miserable will prove otherwise. Others are jealous of other people's expensive belongings, but many expensive items are not even fully paid for and their owners can't sleep for the debt they are in. And some people simply say that money doesn't matter. But let's face it—it's pretty unlikely that such people have ever been in the kind of debt that can follow you around like a black cloud.

So what's the best way to deal with this strange commodity we call money?

Regardless of your salary, you can live comfortably when it comes to money if you regard it as nothing more than a useful tool. Tools are for our convenience. We control them. We think of them only as we need them and we keep them stashed away most of the time. If this is the role you would like money to play in your life, then getting it there is achievable.

Remember that designer shoes aren't likely to make you happy for long, whereas forfeiting them could be the start of a lifetime of financial control and peace of mind. So start making wise decisions today.

"Cut down the role that money (and what it can buy) plays in your life. That way you'll be leaving plenty of space for what really makes you happy..."

index

acknowledgments

I would like to thank my girlfriends—all of whom represent an entire spectrum of approaches toward money—for unwittingly providing the material I needed to write this book. I would like to dedicate this book to my mother who, I have finally conceded, has always been right.